Of Love and War

New & Selected Poems

Also by Vernon Scannell and published by Robson Books:

Poetry
The Loving Game (1975)
New & Collected Poems 1950–1980 (1980)
Winterlude (1982)
Funeral Games (1987)
Soldiering On (1989)
A Time for Fires (1991)
Collected Poems 1950–1993 (1993)

Autobiography
The Tiger and the Rose
A Proper Gentleman
Argument of Kings
Drums of Morning

Fiction
Ring of Truth

Of Love and War
New & Selected Poems

Vernon Scannell

Robson Books

First published in Great Britain in 2002 by Robson Books,
64 Brewery Road, London N7 9NT

A member of Chrysalis Books plc

The author and the publishers have made every
reasonable effort to contact all copyright holders. Any
errors that may have occurred are inadvertent and
anyone who for any reason has not been contacted is
invited to write to the publishers so that a full
acknowledgement may be made in subsequent editions
of this work.

British Library Cataloguing in Publication Data
A catalogue record for this title is available from the
British Library.

ISBN 1 86105 482 3

Typeset by FiSH Books, London WC1
Printed in Great Britain by Mackays of Chatham, Kent

To Jo Peters, with love

Acknowledgements

A few of the previously uncollected poems have appeared in the following literary journals, to the editors of which acknowledgements are due:

AMBIT for 'The Year of the Crab', *Poetry Ireland* for 'Questions about Paradise', *Poetry Review* for 'Old Wounds' and *The Interpreter's House* for 'Love and Courage'.

'Compulsory Mourning' is a slightly revised version of the poem of the same title that was published in *The Black and White Days* (Robson Books,1996).

Contents

Introduction

In my eightieth year and having recently survived a period of hospitalisation with radical treatment for cancer of the throat, I find that my passion for literature in general and poetry in particular, as both reader and practioner, has diminished very little, if at all. That is a cause for grateful rejoicing. What I find less inspiriting is the state of the art of poetry as I see it in the first decade of the twenty-first century. I do not refer here to the vapid doggerel of the 'performance poets' which has always been with us, though not in the past published and rewarded as it is today, but to the advocates of 'poetic disjunction', 'indeterminacy of meaning', 'collage', 'calculated incoherence' and disruption of narrative and syntax, or, to put it plainly, the purveyors of the superficially elegant gibberish that receives serious attention and often high praise from the media and, more shamefully, from the 'serious' critics of academia.

It has been my firm belief since I first began to attempt the art of poetry that the making of a poem should be, as Yeats asserted, a difficult business. However, I have always felt reservations about what seems to me the only partially true belief, stated by both Eliot and Hopkins in their different ways, that the meaning of a poem is of less significance than its structure and texture, Eliot's 'nice bit of meat for the house-dog'. Ideally, the poem should be the perfection of expression of meaning inseparable from the methods by which that expression is achieved. As Paul Valéry has said, 'A man is a poet if the difficulties inherent in his art provide him with ideas; he is not a poet if they deprive him of ideas'.

I believe that far too much of the poetry written in the past four decades or so has differed from prose only in its typo-

1

graphical arrangement on the page and in its being less coherent and harmonious than good prose.

Like most people who try to write poetry I began by trying to imitate the poems which gave me the most pleasure and only gradually came to see that if I was ever going to find a distinctive voice of my own it would be through concentrating on the experience and its furnishings that provided my subject and firmly resolving to tell the truth about what I saw and felt. This quest for poetic truth, I learned, was best pursued by employing the formal devices that had been created and refined by generations of poets from the era of Chaucer to the twentieth century and I became convinced that these shaping principles which had emerged from the practice of great poets helped to prevent the untruths of factitious emotion, bombast and sentimentality from entering the body of the poem.

Quite recently two authors of popular works of modern history, both former war correspondents now working on an account of the Second World War campaign in North Africa, have asked me a number of questions about my experiences in the desert fighting. These questions tended to deal with specific matters of time and place that a detached observer or historian of the period would be better equipped to answer. Keith Douglas, the poet who was killed in Normandy in 1944, has written in his excellent prose book, *Alamein to Zem Zem*, '... what remains in my mind – a flurry of violent impressions – is vivid enough. Against a backcloth of indeterminate landscapes of moods and smells, dance the black and bright incidents'. It is on a similar 'flurry of violent impressions' that I have tried to impose something of the order and coherence of art in a recent poem, *Baptism of Fire*, while making the crucial and ironic point that the civilian, sitting thousands of miles away from the scenes of action, knows far more about the geographical and strategic realities of the events than does the participating common soldier who may well be wounded or killed in the battle.

Not long before writing this account of desert warfare from the viewpoint of a young infantryman I had attempted something rather different, a fictional description of a bomber raid on a German city in which the narrator is the rear-gunner in a crew on its last operation after which its members, should they survive, will be relieved of operational duties. Such technical matters as appear in the poem have been taken from a prose description of a similar raid that I had read in a wartime literary journal. I think I am right in believing that the experience of battle, whether at sea, on land or in the air, is essentially the same and my own tastes of warfare on the ground have made it possible for me to achieve a fairly convincing realisation of what that young gunner felt on his final run.

When I had written the second of these 'war poems' I decided to look back over my earlier work in verse, especially the attempts to deal with the subject of war, and I realised that, first, there was far more of it than I had been aware of accumulating and, second, that the other main theme on which variations have been constantly played was, perhaps unsurprisingly, that of love in its various forms. It was this realisation that suggested to me that I might put together a selection of poems dealing with one or the other, or both, of these themes.

The Year of the Crab, the poem – or perhaps sequence of poems – which ends this volume might seem on first sight out of place among the other pieces whose relation to Eros or Mars, or to both, is more or less direct. I wrote only one small section of *The Year of the Crab* while I was undergoing treatment in Cookridge Oncological Hospital near Leeds (the poem, or episode, called *Night Shift*) but I did make a few notes and thought vaguely that I might write something about the whole experience if and when I was sufficiently recovered. It was only after I had completed the first draft while on a convalescent holiday in Andalusia in the early Spring of 2000 that I came to see that I had written what was, without evading the grimmer aspects of the experience, a kind of celebration of the sustaining power of love.

I hope that readers of contemporary poetry will find that at least a few of the old and new pieces gathered here will provide something in the way of pleasure and even perhaps a little

3

illumination. I have included a variety of moods and forms and I hope devoutly that I have managed to demonstrate to some degree my unshakable belief in, and endorsement of, Keats's words in a letter to his friend Benjamin Bailey: 'I am certain of nothing but the holiness of the heart's affections and the truth of the imagination'.

The Great War

Whenever war is spoken of
I find
The war that was called Great invades the mind:
The grey militia marches over land
A darker mood of grey
Where fractured tree-trunks stand
And shells, exploding, open sudden fans
Of smoke and earth.
Blind murders scythe
The deathscape where the iron brambles writhe;
The sky at night
Is honoured with rosettes of fire,
Flares that define the corpses on the wire
As terror ticks on wrists at zero hour.
These things I see,
But they are only part
Of what it is that slyly probes the heart:
Less vivid images and words excite
The sensuous memory
And, even as I write,
Fear and a kind of love collaborate
To call each simple conscript up
For quick inspection:
Trenches' parapets
Paunchy with sandbags; bandoliers, tin-hats,
Candles in dug-outs,
Duckboards, mud and rats.
Then, like patrols, tunes creep into the mind:

A long long trail, The Rose of No-Man's Land,
Home Fires and Tipperary;
And through the misty keening of a band
Of Scottish pipes the proper names are heard
Like fateful commentary of distant guns:
Passchendaele, Bapaume, and Loos, and Mons.
And now,
Whenever the November sky
Quivers with a bugle's hoarse, sweet cry,
The reason darkens; in its evening gleam
Crosses and flares, tormented wire, grey earth
Splattered with crimson flowers,
And I remember,
Not the war I fought in
But the one called Great
Which ended in a sepia November
Four years before my birth.

Uncle Edward's Affliction

Uncle Edward was colour-blind;
We grew accustomed to the fact.
When he asked someone to hand him
The green book from the window-seat
And we observed its bright red cover
Either apathy or tact
Stifled comment. We passed it over.
Much later, I began to wonder
What curious world he wandered in,
Down streets where pea-green pillar-boxes
Grinned at a fire-engine as green;
How Uncle Edward's sky at dawn
And sunset flooded marshy green.
Did he ken John Peel with his coat so green
And Robin Hood in Lincoln red?
On country walks avoid being stung
By nettles hot as a witch's tongue?
What meals he savoured with his eyes:
Green strawberries and fresh red peas,
Green beef and greener burgundy.
All unscientific, so it seems:
His world was not at all like that,
So those who claim to know have said.
Yet, I believe, in war-smashed France
He must have crawled from neutral mud
To lie in pastures, dark and red
And seen, appalled, on every blade
The rain of innocent green blood.

On Leave: May 1916

And now, at last, after the swollen journey,
Black stubbled hilarity, tobacco reek,
Each sweating hour tumescent with anticipation,
Arrival happens: creak of garden gate,
Fluting and flutters of welcome, kisses and tears,
Sweet and delicate as pomegranate seeds.
Then out of the heat into the shadowed hall;
Dump kit-bag, rifle, webbing; promissory kiss;
Alone, strip off the khaki itch, stiff wool,
The hunks of boot; loll in fragrant mist
Of steam, relax in healing water poured
By those white hands which have, for anxious months,
When idle, clung for comfort each to each.

Listen. Hear the distant tinkling talk
Of cups and saucers, spoons, as feminine
As silver thimbles; those remembered things,
Fragile domesticities, so frail
These symbols; their trivial chatter a language
Of brittle leaves and petals, a simple grammar,
Which voice of barrack-square or trench would shatter.

Now cleansed and dressed in seven-day light disguise
He hides away harsh garments of his calling,
Brown bandages, the leather, steel and brass,
And, looming in the summer parlour, tries
To hide big battering hands, temper his voice
To speakings like breeze-questioned foliage.
He waits.

He has grown used to long and watchful waitings.
When sunlight is withdrawn and dark moves in,
Pickets of stars are posted in the skies;
The scattered natural musics of the day
Are drawn together, patterned as she plays;
The piano smiles beneath her thoughtful hands,
Those clever, sad and crushable bones.

Lamplight spills pools of gold on polished oak,
Bestows a glimmer on her lowered head;
The music falls, lingering, drop by drop,
Into a brimming silence. Her head stays bowed,
And, though he cannot see her eyes, he knows
Their little glitter contradicts the sly
And pensive disavowal of her lips.

All lamps are out; the clock tacks down the dark.
They climb to where the unsurprisable bed
Attends, composed and tolerant witness of
Pale preparations for the tremulous night.
He sees, with awe and pain and gratitude,
In veiling starlight, her quick nakedness
Flash, slender, incandescent, vulnerable,
Before they lie together, move and cling.

In deeper dark he lies in one man's land,
Hears his own voice cry, wounded; far away
The barrage of big guns begins; the flares
Illuminate the sky and show, below,
The crazy scribblings of barbed wire, the fat
Bulges of stacked sand-bags, shattered trees,
The livid stripped forked branches, tangled hair;
Crushed underfoot, the crimson flowers are pulped.
Then rain begins to fall, the dark saps flood;
Salt stings on her bruised mouth; her tears, and his,
Are slow, small rain on dust that turns to mud.

Epithets of War

I
August 1914

The bronze sun blew a long and shimmering call
Over the waves of Brighton and Southend,
Over slapped and patted pyramids of sand,
Paper Union Jacks and cockle stalls;
A pierrot aimed his banjo at the gulls;
Small spades dug trenches to let the channel in
As nimble donkeys followed their huge heads
And charged. In the navy sky the loud white birds
Lolled on no wind, then, swinging breathless, skimmed
The somersaulting waves; a military band
Thumped and brayed, brass pump of sentiment;
And far from the beach, inland, lace curtains stirred.
A girl played Chopin while her sister pored
Over her careful sewing; faint green scent
Of grass was sharpened by a gleam of mint,
And, farther off, in London, horses pulled
Their rumbling drays and vans along the Strand
Or trundled down High Holborn and beyond
The Stadium Club, where, in the wounded world
Of five years later, Georges Carpentier felled
Bulldog Joe Beckett in a single round.
And all is history; its pages smell
Faintly of camphor and dead pimpernel
Coffined in leaves, and something of the sand
And salt of holiday. But dead. The end
Of something never to be lived again.

II
The Guns

A few were preserved years after they had died,
Kept in hushed museums as stuffed animals are;
One, a trench mortar, rested amiably inside
The recreation ground of a midland spa.
The kids took no more notice of it than
The parched fountain or the grass on which they ran.

They were too young to have heard the gun's enormous
    tongue,
Though the blind voice still broke their parents' sleep:
Black sacks of spilled thunder avalanched among
The pastures of dreamed peace; again pacific sheep
Were slaughtered in hot laughter's howl and boom;
Wraiths of dead cordite smelled sweet in the waking
    room.

Dawn tamed the darkness in the skull, put thunder
    down.
Rain slanted hair-thin through the haggard sky;
Again gun-carriages rumbled through the broken town;
Capes gleamed, dark metal, as the infantry marched by.
The guns were silent, but their speakings echoed still:
Anger of names - Cambrai, Bethune, Arras, Kemmel Hill.

Night will surge back, sure as a counter-attack;
Lewis-guns and Vickers will chatter in their fever;
Again the big guns will slam and slash and hack
At silence till it folds about their heads forever;
Then even the names will fade, mere sounds, unbroken
    code,
Marks on the page: Passchendaele, Verdun, The Menin
    Road.

III
Casualties

They were printed daily in the newspapers.
A woman in Nottingham went mad reading them;
She drowned herself in the Trent.
Her name was not included in the casualty lists.

She was mother of two million sons.
At night a frail voice would quaver,
Cry from its bed of mud:
'Stretcher-bearers! Stretcher-bearers!' She could not go.

She could not bear it. Her mind broke.
Barbed-wire scrawled illiterate history
Over the black dough of Belgian fields,
Was punctuated by anatomies.

In Trafalgar Square an English lady
Distributed white feathers among civilians.
Children with sad moustaches and puttee'd calves
Prepared to be translated.

The crazed mother heard them at night
Crying as hot stars exploded
And the earth's belly shook and rumbled
With giant eructations.

The ambulances lurched through the mire in the brain;
Uniformed surgeons in crimson aprons
Laboured at irreparable bodies;
Dawn bristled on their skullish jaws.

And two million of an innocent generation,
Orphaned by a doomed, demented mother,
Unlearned an axiom: they discovered
Only the lucky few meet death once only.

IV
War Songs

A lesson that their children knew by heart
Where it lay stonily in that September.
Conscripted man, anonymous in hot
Brown or blue, intoned his rank and number.
The discs, strung from his neck, no amulet
Against the ache of loss, were worn in darkness
Under grave blankets in the narrow cot
After the bugle's skirmish with night's silence.
In trembling cities civil sleep was probed
By the wild sirens' blind and wounded howling;
White searchlights hosed the sky; black planets throbbed;
At night all buildings put on total mourning.
And, when dawn yawned, the washed skies were afloat
With silver saveloys whose idle motion
And conference with puffed clouds appeared to mock
Bereaving night and morning's lamentation.
And then, down country lanes, the crop-haired sons
And nephews of the skeletons of Flanders
Made seance of their march, as, on their tongues,
The old ghosts sang again of Tipperary,
Packing kit-bags, getting back to Blighty,
But soon, bewildered, sank back to their graves
When others songs were bawled – a jaunty music
With false, bragging words: The Siegfried Line
Transformed with comic washing hanging from it,
Sergeants and Corporals were blessed, the barrel rolled;
But behind the grinning words and steady tramping
The Sergeant of the dark was taking names
And marking time to that lugubrious singing.
We're saying goodbye to them all: and, far away
From gunpit, barrack square and trench, the mother
Sewed the dark garments for tomorrow's mourning.

V
Eidolon Parade

A grey wind prowls across the lake of stone,
The flag flicks like a summer horse's tail,
The brass voice of the bugle climbs and clings
High before it crumbles, falls and fades.
CSM Hardy, back from Salerno Beach,
Glitters with sea salt, winkles nest in his eyes,
But his voice grinds loud as ever as he calls
The Nominal Roll: Corporal Mick McGuire
Has returned from Alamein, each orifice
Is clogged with sand; but tonight he will appear
Once more at the Church Hall, battle-dress pressed
And patent leather highlights on his feet;
And when the lights are dimmed, the last waltz makes
Its passionate interrogation: *Who's
Taking You Home Tonight?* who but McGuire,
Although his terrible kiss will taste of sand
Gritting on shocked teeth, and his cold cheek
Will seem to her a stony reprimand.
And, while the Corporal tangoes, Private Bain,
A bunch of quarrels hanging from each wrist,
Will sluice his guts with twenty black-and-tans;
But he stands still now, sober, at attention
With that small company paraded there
Waiting for inspection: Dodger Rae,
Equipment scruffy and an idle bootlace,
Is put on an eternal two-five-two;
Spike Liston, gaunt as a Belsen boy or saint,
Still rages for more grub; Bull Evans broods
On all the thighs he'll never lie between
Or lie about, his pack and pouches stuffed
With fantasies and condoms; Les King, who crooned
Like Bing, is back from Mareth where he lay,
The tunes mislaid, gargling with his blood.

His songs are out of date. And there are others
Whose faces, though familiar, fade and blur.
The bugle publishes another cry.
Two more commands explode; butts and boots
Crash and ring; another echoing shout
And, by the left, they start to march away.
The steady tramping dims into a mist.
The stone ground stretches in its vacancy;
One final flick of flag, the mist comes down,
And silence stuns with its enormous weight,
And there is nothing left to do but sleep.

Walking Wounded

A mammoth morning moved grey flanks and groaned.
In the rusty hedges pale rags of mist hung;
The gruel of mud and leaves in the mauled lane
Smelled sweet, like blood. Birds had died or flown,
Their green and silent attics sprouting now
With branches of leafed steel, hiding round eyes
And ripe grenades ready to drop and burst.
In the ditch at the cross-roads the fallen rider lay
Hugging his dead machine and did not stir
At crunch of mortar, tantrum of a Bren
Answering a Spandau's manic jabber.
Then into sight the ambulances came,
Stumbling and churning past the broken farm,
The amputated sign-post and smashed trees,
Slow wagonloads of bandaged cries, square trucks
That rolled on ominous wheels, vehicles
Made mythopoeic by their mortal freight
And crimson crosses on the dirty white.
This grave procession passed, though, for a while,
The grinding of their engines could be heard,
A dark noise on the pallor of the morning,
Dark as dried blood; and then it faded, died.
The road was empty, but it seemed to wait –
Like a stage which knows a cast is in the wings –
Wait for a different traffic to appear.
The mist still hung in snags from dripping thorns;
Absent-minded guns still sighed and thumped.

And then they came, the walking wounded,
Straggling the road like convicts loosely chained,
Dragging at ankles exhaustion and despair.
Their heads were weighted down by last night's lead,
And eyes still drank the dark. They trailed the night
Along the morning road. Some limped on sticks;
Others wore rough dressings, splints and slings;
A few had turbanned heads, the dirty cloth
Brown-badged with blood. A humble brotherhood,
Not one was suffering from a lethal hurt,
They were not magnified by noble wounds,
There was no splendour in that company.
And yet, remembering after eighteen years,
In the heart's throat a sour sadness stirs;
Imagination pauses and returns
To see them walking still, but multiplied
In thousands now. And when heroic corpses
Turn slowly in their decorated sleep
And every ambulance has disappeared
The walking wounded still trudge down that lane,
And when recalled they must bear arms again.

Baptism of Fire

He is no kid. He's nineteen and he's tough,
a hard man like Maclaren who, it's true,
is getting on in years and has three stripes,
and three kids, too, at home in civvy street;
but Sergeant Mac's a tough guy through and through:
he'll see them right when things get really rough.

They reach the starting-line in night's disguise.
It isn't fear exactly that he feels:
excitement, certainly, and something else,
a small black living thing inside his gut
that grows and squirms as sudden livid weals
are slashed across the dark face of the skies.

And, with the flashes, swollen thunder roars
as, from behind, the barrage of big guns
begins to batter credence with its din
and, overhead, death whinnies for its feed
while countering artillery shakes and stuns
with slamming of a million massive doors.

The iron fever of machine-gun fire –
more intimate but no less menacing –
spits tracers through the dark; his teeth begin
to chatter in spontaneous mimicry.
Flares' phosphorescent dahlias climb and cling.
His Company moves forward to the wire.

Beyond the wire the sand is sown with mines,
but Sappers have been there to cut a track
of safety through that zone of murderous tricks,
though if death doesn't burst from underfoot
it whistles through the air and can attack
from any angle and at any time.

Now shells and mortar-bombs explode around
and hurl dry geysers of detritus high;
he smells and tastes the fierce sweet bitterness
of cordite's pagan incense, then he hears
not far ahead, through mangled air, a cry —
a frail, yet weirdly penetrating sound:

at first unrecognised and meaningless,
a wordless wail, and then crude parody
of Sergeant Mick Maclaren's normal voice,
or what that voice might sound like if the man
were gelded or flung back to infancy,
a querulous sound of babyish distress.

Then words emerge: 'Oh mother! Mother! Please!
Oh Jesus Christ! Oh ma!' Grotesque, obscene.
After the first bewildering shock he feels
vicarious shame, a sense, too, of betrayal.
And then a shell's explosion intervenes:
blast knocks him grovelling to his contrite knees.

That voice has died away but echoes stain
a corner of his brain as others cry
for stretcher-bearers or God's aid, while he
is quite alone and lost, as they all are.
Old men at breakfast might know where and why
he's where he is—it's called El Alamein.

The Bombing of the Café de Paris, 1941

Snakehips, the bandleader, wore a gallant grin,
A clip of white cartridges; he and the boys
Tapped natty polished toes to keep the time
Of tango, quickstep, foxtrot, blues and swing;
The basement of the place was deep and safe,
No other-ranks or bombs would be let in.

A boy in Air Force blue danced with his mother;
A sub-lieutenant stroked his girl's silk knee;
Caressing lights lay soft on hair and flesh,
Bright on badges, deep in polished leather.
A major of the Black Watch called for Scotch
And winked at his admiring younger brother.

Oh Johnny, Oh Johnny, how you can love,
That was the song they liked. They could forget
That loving wasn't all that he must do:
Oh Johnny, Oh Johnny, heavens above –
And in the hidden heavens the siren's wailing
Mourned over London and the shattered dove.

But no one there could hear. The music gushed
And wine corks popped like children's wooden guns.
No warning when the bomb came bursting in,
Huge knuckle-dustered fist that struck and crushed
Furniture of wood and flesh; the bang's
Enormous shadow paled; the place was hushed.

Some light remained, and from the ceiling came
Floating down a fine cosmetic dust
That settled softly on the hair and skin
Of the sailor's girl, who, wholly without shame,
Sprawled in ripped clothes, one precious stocking gone
And with it half her leg. No one would blame

Her carelessness for once, and if they did
She would not care. The sailor lay beneath
Dark flood of fallen curtain, quiet and still,
As if he rested on the ocean bed.
The airman's mother sat upon the floor,
Crooned comfort to her child's deaf cradled head.

Snakehips had put away his grin forever.
Music might return, but he would not.
The kilted major found another drink
Then carried out his brother, like an order,
Joining the stunned survivors in the street,
Sick from their meeting with the dark marauder.

While, down below, a woman lay and saw
A man approaching through the powdery gloom;
She could not move trapped limbs. 'Rescue!' she thought
As by her side he knelt upon the floor,
Reached out to finger at her neck and take
Her string of pearls in one triumphant paw.

Outside, the sirens once again composed
A mocking dirge above the crouching town;
Along the blackened streets on nervous wheels
The blinkered ambulances gently nosed,
Ferrying cool instruments of mercy.
An incident of war was almost closed.

The Final Run

Huddled in his perspex world he sees
the other, night-swathed, world fall far below
and feels the engines of the Lancaster
settle to their steady humming drone
as, on the intercom, he hears the wheeze
and crackle of the static, then the cool,
smart-blazered public school tones of the skipper
checking on each member of the crew:
'Pilot to rear-gunner: all okay?'
He answers, 'Okay Skipper,' as he grips
the trips that swing his turret to and fro
from one side to the other, high and low,
quartering the sky in anxious search
for bristling predators, the Messerschmitts
and Junkers that could smash them from their perch
on shifty air and make their final run
the last indeed.
                          This is his thirtieth raid
and then no more. Six months on cosy ground,
a cushy job instructing rookies, then,
with luck, the war would be kaput and he
need never suffer this ordeal again.

His final run: he shivers in his sweat
and, rising, peers below to see the faint
pale thread of surf that marks the Belgian coast
and knows ack-ack will soon begin to vent
its vivid rage in pyrotechnic show

of shells and tracers he has seen before
so many times and, minutes later, those
black branches far beneath begin to flower
in brilliant blossomings that flash and blaze.
He speaks into his mike; his throat is sore,
tongue thick with thirst: 'Gunner to pilot. Flak —
starboard quarter down!'
                          He feels his seat
fall away beneath him as the plane
dives and for a moment leaves him there,
breathless and suspended in the air,
before it levels and soars up again,
re-seating him, and then gets back on course.

The lethal firework show is left behind
and moonless night is smeared across his sight.
He stares into the murk and hopes to find
no moving menace there of any kind,
but almost instantly he is aware
of something flicking, quicker than a tick,
across his stare. It disappears, then zooms
distinctly into view – the vicious, slick
and hammer-headed Junkers 88
moving into kill – and for one sick,
engulfing second he, and he alone,
is quivering, mortal target for that flight
of stinging tracers which he knows will soon
whizz sizzling through the night, all aiming for
his heartjammed, throbbing throat.
                          His voice is hoarse:
'One Jerry fighter! starboard quarter down!
One thousand yards – prepare to corkscrew soon!'
                          Death closes in,
expelling its thin stream
of evil brilliants as the gunner roars,
'Eight hundred yards! . . . now six! . . . five hundred! . . . –
    Go!'

and presses his own triggers, sees the foe
bank and twist and slide away below
to leave the sky impassive as before.
He gasps out, 'Break away!'
                    The pilot's voice
replies, 'Good lad, but keep a sharp lookout.
He might be back again.'
                    And on they drone
until they are again saluted by
the flash and crack of ack-ack fire and fierce
blades of probing light thrust up to pierce
the scarred and trembling fabric of the night.
The plane is shaken, bounced, but on it flies
above the stricken city lit by fires
from earlier bombs. 'We're over target now!'
Bomb-aimer's voice: 'Left!...Steady!...Left again
and steady!...Bombs away! Okay!...Okay!...
Steady for incendiaries...they're gone!...
Let's get the hell away from here! Let's run!'

The aircraft with its quivering cargo veers
away to starboard, turns and heads for home.
The gunner stares through perspex at the crazed
astronomy of searchlight dazzle, flares
and tracers, shellbursts and infernal glow
from razed and burning buildings down below
and prays no fighters will swoop into view
to make the 'final' of their final trip
irreversibly and mercilessly true.
'For Christ's sake don't relax. We've come too far
to get the chop tonight!' The skipper's voice
is less urbane, democratised by fear.
The gunner grins but knows that his own voice,
should he speak now, would be as strained and hoarse,
if not far worse.
                    And then the aircraft bucks

and lurches as the blast from shellburst lifts
it tilting for long seconds and he hears
quick shrapnel rattle on the fuselage
and knows their corporate terror will not brook
denial or attempts at camouflage,
and all the crew is muttering spells or prayers.
                                        And they survive.
The Lancaster drones on beyond the reach
of anti-aircraft fire, the naked flares
and questing jets of incandescent light.
Their target's crematorial glow recedes
and dims before it's swallowed by their flight.
Below, land melts away, becomes the sea,
and then the gunner dares, almost, to say
that they will make it, though he's often heard
grim tales of aircraft shot down close to base.
His throat is swollen now, his tongue warm-furred
and eyes feel like hot cinders, vision blurred.
The pilot speaks: his smooth tones, now restored,
sound casual and confident again:
'All right rear-gunner? Are you still awake?'

The plane is circling now. The gunner's grin
comes slow but wide: 'I'm fine. A piece a cake!'

Compulsory Mourning

'M. described his treatment of tank commanders who had lost crews and were unwilling to command another tank as "compulsory mourning". He arranged for them "...to be confined to a small darkened room for three days with an order to mourn" and blunt statements were made about their selfishness...they were fed on water and bread alone and were allowed one hour's daylight and one hour's electric light a day.'

From a report on 'The Northfield Experiment', a survey of psychiatric treatment given to soldiers in Northfield Military Hospital, Birmingham 1940–47.

I lie in darkness on this bed of stone.
The shrewd cold bites like acid to the bone
And I am sick with gelded rage and hate,
And something else I can't quite designate,
A bitter taste, like guilt. And then the flood
Of concentrated loathing, dark as blood
Surges through me and it leaves behind,
Among the sludge and lumber in the mind,
An image, vast and vivid, of his face,
Plump, well-shaven, showing not a trace
Of doubt or sympathy, this man who claims
That he's not hoodwinked by my little games,
And sees with X-ray eyes through walls of bone
Inside the haunted skull, and he alone
Can teach me how to mourn as I should do
The charred and blackened things that were my crew.

I think of his soft hands, like pastry dough,
And how they'd spit and sizzle in the glow
Inside the turret of a brewed-up tank.

Yesterday he said, 'I'll be quite frank.
You men are selfish shits – I see you grin!
All you can think of is your precious skin!
Well I am here to bring you to your senses
And find a way to break through those defences
That you have built, no doubt unconsciously,
Against accepting what is clear to me:
To mourn your former crew would mean that you
Must face mortality as something true,
Not just the death of others, but your own.
You can't admit we all must die alone.
All right. I grant the treatment might appear
A little harsh, but let me make this clear:
It's not a punishment although it may,
To you, seem not so different, shall we say,
From doing Solitary at Aldershot.
You'll be confined in darkness and we'll not
Allow you more than two hours' light each day.
You'll be on bread and water. There you'll stay
For three full days and nights and we shall find,
I think, that this will concentrate the mind
Quite wonderfully, as Dr Johnson said.
In there you'll find a way to mourn your dead.'

And he, of course, is wrong as he could be.
The dead are dead and mean no more to me
Than I to them. Though wait! I must admit
There's something else to say, and this is it:
The dead can't smell themselves – at least I pray
To Christ they can't! How terrible if they
not only have to bear, but be their smell
For evermore in some peculiar hell!

That smell is in my nostrils, seems to spread
Inside my mouth and throat, it's in my head.
And with it come the voices of the war,
The glint of pain and terror through the roar
Of our Crusader's engine and the shrill
Static, morse and jamming noise that spill
From radio to season this rich din;
And, from outside, the almost childish, thin
Rattle of machine guns and blunt thud
Of eighty-eights. And then the tune of blood,
A soft insistent note, a kind of sigh
That lingers when the other voices die
And is ubiquitous. It joins the scent
Of cooking human flesh, is redolent
Of war and all that means, and ever meant.

In my protracted night the hours are melled
Into a timeless slur and I am held
By links of frozen minutes to a stake
Of impotence and anger. Though awake
I can't escape the images and sounds
That rise from nightmare's heaving burial grounds.
But I'll survive. And, furthermore, *his* scorn
And punitive attempts to make me mourn
The cinders of my crew will never crack
This resolution never to go back
And do it all again. In just three days
I'll rise from here and walk into the blaze
Of morning sunshine like the third day lad,
The Son of Man, and I shall swear I've had
A change of heart, that now my single aim
Is vengeance on the swine who are to blame
For my dead comrades' fate. Then he will claim
A medical and military success,
And he'll be wrong again. My readiness
To soldier on will be a trickster's act,

But he'll be fooled and swallow it as fact,
Hooked by his vanity. As for my crew,
I'm sure they'd both endorse my point of view.
I see them now: Chalky, my driver, hard
Middleweight from Bethnal Green, with scarred
Eyebrows, flattened nose, and such a flow
Of hoarse profanity you'd never know
That he was just nineteen and that below
The carapace of toughness you would find
A gentleness surprising as the mind
That in the worst of crises understood
The situation as I rarely could;
He'd grunt his practical advice although
He never let a glimpse of smugness show,
Nor hinted that he thought that he should be
Commander of the tank instead of me.
The gunner, Jim, complete antithesis
Of Chalky but, maybe because of this,
His steadfast mucker, rarely said a word
And, when he did, the tone of voice you heard
Was mild as butter, mellow from the green
Devon hills and fields, the words as clean
As Sunday linen though, when we attacked,
Or were ourselves attacked, he would react
With steely competence and seem to be
A cool extension of the gun that he
With steady concentration aimed and fired.

And now, the man who thinks he hold a key
To wind his soldiers up and then decree
That they be used again in lethal games
Must be dismissed as, in the dark, your names
Chalky and Jim, turn slowly in my mind,
Those unburnt syllables. I hope I'll find
A way to make them breathe. Meanwhile I try
To coax oblivion to where I lie

And roll between my forefinger and thumb
A piece of bread, no bigger than a crumb,
Until it is an amuletic ball
With magic properties that might forestall
Invasion of those images which maul
The unprotected consciousness when sleep
Takes full command and I no longer keep
My regimental mask secure, in place,
And wake at dawn to find my human face
Smeared and wet with tears. *He* must not see
That shameful nakedness exposed, for he
Would claim success for his experiment.
Being as stupid as malevolent
He would not know, nor would he ever know
Those saline exclamation-marks don't show
My mourning, as he understands the word –
No impulse to avenge will have occurred –
Just speechless sorrow as the grit of guilt
That can't, however many tears are spilt,
Be washed away. I shall not fight again.
There are no accusations from the slain,
Nor will there ever be; yet, when that's said,
The spirits or the shadows of the dead
Must be petitioned and appeased. I pray
Into the unresponsive dark that they,
My better, braver, comrades will forgive
Not just this unheroic urge to live
(Small doubt of that) but chiefly this regret
That I must bear the burden and the boon
Of living on beyond their brief forenoon.
I think that they would wish me to rejoice
Without regret and would approve my choice
Of opting for old age in civvy street.
I hope that's so.

I don't suppose we'll meet
In some celestial boozer later on,
But one thing is for sure: when I have gone
From this infernal place I may well find
Myself not drinking at, but stuck behind,
Bars of the uncongenial, penal kind.
But I'll get out and then I'll drink to you
Chalky and Jim – and this I hope is true:
As long as I am able to survive,
While I still breathe, I'll keep you two alive.

Perimeter Guard

His second two-hour duty: the wind
Is now stropped to such
Fine and steely sharpness that
It might slice off a shrivelled lobe or finger.
The stars are brilliant chippings of frozen flint,
Beautiful, but quite indifferent
To sublunar hurt.

His stunned toes are welded together;
He is club-footed
By the weather. The only
Nostrum for such misery and loneliness
Is found in fantasies of somewhere other,
A feminine place, not erotic
But warm, motherly.

Lavender-scented pillow and sheets;
No gruff blankets there:
Soft wool, a cool counterpane
Of candlewick that soothed an infant fever;
Sweet, unsnoring dark. He shuts his eyes against
The stars' impersonal derision
And the wind's malice.

Then dream and the silence are broken
By a sound beyond
The wire and his eyes are filled
With star-sparks like frozen tears; unsure he calls
'Halt! Who goes there?' No one answers. The glitter
Melts from his eyes; then he hears the wind
Whisper: 'Foe!...Foe!...Foe!...'

Casualty – Mental Ward

Something has gone wrong inside my head.
The sappers have left mines and wire behind,
I hold long conversations with the dead.

I do not always know what has been said;
The rhythms, not the words, stay in my mind;
Something has gone wrong inside my head.

Not just the sky but grass and trees are red,
The flares and tracers – or I'm colour-blind;
I hold long conversations with the dead.

Their presence comforts and sustains like bread;
When they don't come it's hard to be resigned;
Something has gone wrong inside my head.

They know about the snipers that I dread
And how the world is booby-trapped and mined;
I hold long conversations with the dead;

As all eyes close, they gather round my bed
And whisper consolation. When I find
Something has gone wrong inside my head
I hold long conversations with the dead.

Sentences

Soldiers serving sentences in Military Prisons and Detention Barracks are officially referred to and addressed as S.U.S's – Soldiers Under Sentence.

Who spiked the water at the wedding
   Held in the Sergeant's Mess?
We all know who the fellow was:
          Jay...
          E...
          S.U.S!

Who blew reveille in the dead man's ear,
   Made him get up and dress?
It wasn't the Company Bugler, but
          Jay...
          E...
          S.U.S!

Who fed the whole battalion
   On one man's rations ? Guess!
Of course you know; it could only be
          Jay...
          E...
          S.U.S!

Who marched across the sea, his boots
  Bright and dry? Why, Yes!
The smartest man in the Regiment:
              Jay...
              E...
              S.U.S!

Who made the tempest halt, ground arms
  And stand at ease, no less ?
The man who knew the word of command –
              Jay...
              E...
              S.U.S!

Who rode a donkey into town
  And cried in his distress?
We don't know why, but we know who:
              Jay...
              E...
              S.U.S!

Who chased the Pay Corps scroungers from
  The place of holiness;
Bashed spuds on Sunday? Who but he,
              Jay...
              E...
              S.U.S!

Who woke the colonel's daughter from
  Death's sleep to wakefulness ?
Not Sawbones but the miracle lad,
              Jay...
              E...
              S.U.S!

Who ripped night's bandage from the eyes
  And healed men's sightlessness?
It wasn't the MO's orderly but
                    Jay...
                    E...
                    S.U.S!

Who never wore a pip or stripe
  Yet still achieved success?
Who held the lowest rank of all?
                    Jay...
                    E...
                    S.U.S!

Who got beat up by Itie cops
  To force him to confess?
Who got put on a Two-five-two?[1]
                    Jay...
                    E...
                    S.U.S!

Who took the Redcaps'[2] fists and boots,
His face a bloody mess
And then got taken out to die?
                    Jay...
                    E...
                    S.U.S!

Who swallowed wine and pissed out water,
Couldn't wake up when reveille was blown,
Who screwed Colonel Jairus's daughter,
Ate ten men's rations, all on his own,
Robbed the blind and beat up cripples,
Flogged his donkey right to the bone?

Johnny Evans, he was the fellow,
Ended up high against the bloodshot sky,
Johnny Evans, the barrack-room cowboy,
Arms stretched out like a PTI[3]
He, and another old Janker-wallah,
One each side of the man who cried
A loud reproach to his stone-deaf father
And promised Johnny, before he died,
A place that night in the Officer's Mess,
He, Johnny Evans, was a Soldier Under Sentence
                    Jay...
                    E...
                    S.U.S!

---

[1]   The Army Charge-sheet
[2]   Military Police
[3]   Physical Training Instructor

Cows in Red Pasture

Last summer in a Kentish field
I saw the plush green darkened by
A whim of light and darkened too
By whiteness of the sheep which stood
Diminished by the distance so
They looked like gravestones on the green,
So still and small and white they seemed.
As this warm memory blurs and fades,
The emptiness bequeathed instructs
Me, curiously, to resurrect
An older memory of a field
Which I would rather far forget:
A foreign field, a field of France,
In which there lay two cows, one white
With maps of black stamped on its hide,
The other just the colour of
The caramel that I once loved.
Both were still; the toffee one
Lay on its back, its stiff legs stuck
Up from the swollen belly like
A huge discarded set of bagpipes.
The piebald cow lay on its side
Looking like any summer beast
Until one saw it had no head.

The grass on which they lay was red.

Remembering the Dead at Wadi Akarit

The Millennium slithers to its close. A haggard December
damages the daylight; the bruised sky lours,
then darkness drapes the town though, in the Square,
the patient clock denies that this is night.

The old man gazes through an upstairs window-pane
over polished tiles and lemon lozenges of light
to where the town becomes an orange-tinted glow
against the sky. Thunder mutters like an afterthought.

This rumbling, though, reminds his mouth and throat
of a sharp, blue bitter-sweetness in stunned air
and slips a still-fresh picture in the window-frame,
replacing the orange-smeared darkness there.

He sees the shapes of rock, the sand and rubble
on which, at unshaven dawn, the bodies sprawl
or lie with unpurposed and tidy decorum,
all neat in battle-order and KD uniform.

Disposed in their scattered dozens like fragments
of a smashed whole, each human particle
is almost identical, rhyming in shape and pigment,
all, in their mute eloquence, oddly beautiful.

As the sun strengthens, a faint sweet feculence spreads.
Dark birds wheel and soar. Fresh light applies
a maquillage of ochre and red. Furtive needs
and greeds begin to plunder the submissive dead.

The old man's eyelids flutter. He shakes his head.
The picture holds, then fades and slowly disappears
with cordite-breath and the pungent sweetness of the dead.
What stays is the shade of the unforgiving years.

Robbie

They all had a job to do in the platoon:
Mortar, rifle, One and Two on the Bren,
Or Section Leader with the light and lucky Sten.
But they also had their other parts to play:
Each of them chose a special role to act –
Walker, a gormless youth; Bill Gray, the buffoon;
Gordon Rennie, the world's pet uncle; Micky Rae,
A slash-lipped gangster; Davis, the rebel who attacked
All stout authority behind its Sam-Browned back.
Robbie alone played no part but his own:
Cotton-haired, potato-faced, he couldn't even say
What time it was; impossible to tell
How much he felt. Too dumb to act the clown,
With eyes like two dud flashlamp bulbs
He grinned a lot, seemed happy as a rule.

Near Caen, the day before the big attack,
Davis was heard to mutter to Bill Gray,
'Robbie's the lucky one who's not scared stiff.
He'll be all right. He can't tell night from day.
He's less imagination than my pack.
I envy him, I don't mind telling you.'
And Bill agreed. That night they got pinned down
By Moaning Minnies. Seven at a time
Those mortar bombs howled over, all night through.
It seemed impossible that anyone would live
But when the morning came things weren't too bad.
They checked their losses – only three were dead,

Among them Robbie. Clever for once, he had
Sucked on his rifle-muzzle like a straw
And somehow blown away most of his head.

El Alamein: 50th Anniversary, October 1992

Fifty years! He's old and out of sorts
But still he smiles to see them on the screen,
The lads they were, tin hats, enormous shorts
As big as bivouacs. Full magazine,
One up the spout, going in at the high-port
Through smoke, a newsreel shot in black and white;
A fake for civvies, so he'd always thought;
It wasn't cameras shooting that first night.

And then live interviews – well, just about –
Old men, false teeth and medals, pretty toys
Dangling from their ribbons. Gaunt or stout
They wheeze or croak. Fade out. He hears the noise
Of bugle's rhetoric; then words: *Lest we forget.*
He snorts; then wonders why his face is wet.

War Movie Veteran

You can't tell me a thing that I don't know
About combat, son. I reckon I've seen them all
On the big screen or TV, the late-night show
Or Sunday matinee. I'm what you'd call
An old campaigner; some of them I've seen
Four-five times maybe. I've got so's I
Can tell for sure which ones among that green
Platoon of rookies are the guys to die.
You know the sensitive and quiet kid
Who can't stand rough stuff, says his prayers at night
And never cusses? He's got to wind up dead
But not before we've seen that he can fight
And he's got guts. He ain't afraid to kill
Once the chips are down. The one to see
Turn really yellow is the loud-mouthed mother
That talks like he ain't scared of nothing; he
Will go, expendable. So will the other,
The black guy who's as good as you or me,
And the Jew that's seeking vengeance for his brother.
The comedian – the hero's buddy – could
Come through the battle in one piece or not:
He's only there for laughs, that's understood
By veterans like me. The hero's got
To be alive and kicking at the end.
The one I really like – you know the guy
The tough top-sergeant, nobody's best friend,
His favourite meal is bullets, blood and rye;
The Krauts he's killed is anybody's guess.

He's made of steel and leather, but you'll find
That he can be the soul of gentleness
With scared old ladies, babies and the blind
Pooch whose master's been knocked off. But never
Think the guy's gone soft: back under fire
He's just as cold and murderous as ever,
He's everything a General could desire.
He'll come through safe okay.
                                                    I tell you, son,
I could write out the list of casualties
Long before the battle has begun.
I've seen it all. I know the way it is
And got to be. Well, that's what you could call
The human side, psychology I guess.
The other stuff – a cinch to learn it all
In half-a-dozen battles, maybe less.
It takes no time to get the different ranks:
Enlisted men and noncoms, officers,
The names of hardware, ammunition, tanks
And how the thing is planned. You'll think at first
That war is chaos, howl of bullet, shell
And bomb; flashes and thunder as they burst,
Flying shit, hot jig-saw bits of hell.
Not so. It's all worked out before the start.
It's choreographed, like in a dance, okay?
You get to know the pattern. War's an art,
It's one I understand. There ain't no way
That you'll find anyone to tell you more
Than me about realities of war.

Bush Vet

That's what they call me. Know what it means?
A veteran of Nam, that's vee-et-nam,
You might have heard of it. It's history now.
The bush, that's where I live,
Up there. You see the trees against the sky,
The forest on the hillside like a pelt?
That's home for me,
Miles away from any living soul.
I come down here
Maybe once a month, or less than that,
To get supplies, oil for the lamp,
Coffee, cans of beans and stuff,
Whisky and tobacco, chiefly them.
A couple, maybe three times, in a year
I get to come in here and hang one on,
Not for company you understand.
I don't get lonely in the bush.
It's other folk, like those guys over there,
That make you feel the loneliness come down.
No sir, I got no need of company,
I like it fine up there.
When I first picked the place
So long ago,
I can't recall exactly when,
I fixed a kind of bivouac.
I slept in that while building me a shack.
It took a while but I'd got time enough.
It don't look great, but keeps the weather out,
And other things. There's memories of Nam

I just can't talk about. Bad things.
I think a lot and sometimes I read books,
That's when I'm feeling tidy in my head,
When I can concentrate. Mostly though
I dream about what was and might have been.
But here's a crazy thing I'll tell you now:
After I got back from Nam
And got my discharge, tried to settle down,
I couldn't make it. Mostly couldn't sleep
And if I did, oh man, the dreams I had.
But here's the crazy part. I missed it all.
I wanted to get back – well, part of me –
I dreamed about the palm groves and the paddies,
The water buffalo, the bamboo hills,
The wooden ploughs the oxen used to pull,
The peasants working in the fields,
The elephant grass that sliced you like a knife,
The leeches, mud and shit, the fear.
Even that.
I got depressed, got mad. I couldn't help it.
Couple a drinks and I could kill,
Kill anyone you understand.
I had to get away.
I'm safe up there.
There's water near my shack, a stream.
I don't need halizone for that.
Truth is I'm just not fit for anything,
I mean for living in a city,
Or anywhere with ordinary folk.
I seen too many killed, too many kids
And women, little children, cooked alive.
I seen too much. I need to clean my eyes,
My hands as well. I never will.
In the bush up there I'm safe, I'm tame.
If any human being does get shot
That person will be me. By friendly fire.

That's what they called it when a guy
Got wasted by a buddy's careless stray.
They called it friendly fire.
It happened all the time. And what the hell
Difference does it make, a VC slug
Or M14, you end up dead the same.
I sometimes wish I had.
There's some things I don't want to ask myself,
And yet the questions sneak up in the night
And grab you by the throat. Or should I say
The question there's no hiding from.
What was it for?
The killing and the fear, the suffering, the shit?
What was it for? And if the question's bad
The answer's worse. Nothing. That's the word.
You know what nothing is?
Nothing is a hole with nothing in it,
A round black emptiness with nothing round it,
A hole punched in a human skull,
When all the flesh has rotted, gone.
Nothing is the muzzle of a gun,
Dark centre of a whirlpool made of steel,
The dark beyond the dark.
Emptiness beyond all emptiness,
Silence under silence,
Nothing is the answer to it all.

Love and Courage

When Barnes, the beefy bully, ambushed him
while crossing Casey's Field that afternoon
heading from school for home's safe certainty,
he howled for pity, but was given none.
The pain he felt was nothing to the shame
of weak submission he was dirtied by.
Fear paralysed; he couldn't even run.

Ten years later, when war's thunder rolled
and cloud-sacks spilled fierce hail of fire and steel,
he was compelled to put on uniform
and learn to dish out death. He could conceal
his terror till his Company was called
to face real battle's homicidal storm.
He chose desertion, ignominy and jail.

That is, if choice existed, which I doubt.
When nervous 'peace' was finally restored
he was released, but still found much to fear.
If accident or argument occurred
in street or square he quickly turned about
and walked the other way. Yet he'd declare
the charge of cowardice to be absurd.

His conduct was determined, he maintained,
by what he was – imaginative, kind,
and sensitive. His nature, never made
for deeds of derring-do, had been designed
for art and tenderness. Yet, in the end,
he failed there, too; for love and courage need
the selfless heart, by which both are defined.

Old Wounds

Long ago the wounds were healed,
and he forgets that they once bled
and burned and blotted out the light
and sumptuous colours of the world,
and filled his unprotected head
with loud but wordless night.

Now each wound quietly lies below
its dark or silver cicatrice
and does not hurt at all, unless
the weather turns and bleak winds blow
with threats, or their fulfilment, of
unpitying hail and snow.

Then pain, or its pale phantom, haunts
the places where it left its prints;
but other kinds of hurt occur:
a half-forgotten tune or scent
can penetrate, and slyly stir
long dormant shades of her.

As when, two days ago, he saw
her cross the street; and there she stood,
her smile against the sun, half-frown,
a look that he had always loved.
Then she was gone. The wound wept raw,
and words seeped out like blood.

Love

Is it like a carnival with spangles and balloons,
Fancy-dress and comic masks and sun-drenched afternoons
Without a cloud to spoil the blue perfection of the skies?
'Well yes, at first, but later on it might seem otherwise. '

Is it like a summer night when stock and roses stain
The silken dark with fragrance and the nightingale again
Sweetly pierces silence with its silver blades of song?
'I say once more it can be thus, but not for very long.'

Is it like a great parade with drums and marching feet
And everybody cheering them, and dancing in the street,
With laughter swirling all around and only tears of joy?
'If that alone, you'd find the fun would soon begin to cloy.'

Is it like the falling snow, noiseless through the night;
Mysterious as moonlight and innocent and bright,
Changing the familiar world with its hypnotic spell?
'It has been known to be like that, and other things as well.

'But if you find, when all the brightest ribbons have grown frayed,
The colours faded, music dumb, and all that great parade
Dismissed into the darkness where the moon has been put out,
Together you find warmth and strength, then that's what it's about.'

Why?

They ask me why I love my love. I say,
'Why do summer's roses smell so sweet
And punctually put on their rich display?

'Why does winter lash the fields with sleet
And make cold music in the leafless trees
Yet strangely seem to warm our snug retreat?

'Why does moody April taunt and tease
With alternating sun and dancing rain?
Why do nettles sting the flesh like bees?

'Why are the stars tonight like silver grain
Broadcast on the far dark fields of sky?
Why does the owl rehearse its sad refrain?

'With loving, too: no point in asking why.
There is no answer.' That is my reply.

The Power of Love

It can alter things:
The stormy scowl can become
Suddenly a smile.

The knuckly bunched fist
May open like a flower,
Tender a caress.

Beneath its bright warmth
Black ice of suspicion melts;
Danger is dazzled.

A plain and dull face
Astounds with its radiance
And sudden beauty.

Ordinary things –
Teacups, spoons and sugar-lumps –
Become magical.

The locked door opens;
Inside are leaves and moonlight;
You are welcomed in.

Its delicate strength
Can lift the heaviest heart
And snap hostile steel.

It gives eloquence
To the dumb tongue, makes plain speech
Blaze like poetry.

Love in Any City

It could have been any city – London, Rome,
Paris, New York, Chicago – any home
For simmering crowds and parks and monoliths
Pocked with a hundred peeping squares, where myths
Proliferate against the darkening sky
In brilliant beads of light or, in the sly
And sweetened shadows, joggle on a screen;
A place where the poor and sick are rarely seen
But covered up like sores, where the air is rich,
Spiced and spiked to aggravate the itch
Of need for what one can't or dare not say.
She seemed the City's child in every way:
No wimpled pretty, stroking her sad lyre,
Impatient for her silver-plated squire,
She couldn't show that soft pre-raphaelite
Hair that syrups smoothly over white
Marmoreal shoulders, neither were her eyes
Those wistful jellies of astounding size;
And yet, though many might not notice it,
Her gaze reflected sympathy and wit
In such a way that it could claim a kind
Of magic that obscurely undermined
His selfish palisades. And though both used
A taut elliptic idiom which refused
A melting welcome to the lyric or
Enraptured paean, by which they set small store,

When streets were hushed, swept bare by the night's
    smooth broom,
A meadow breeze swayed cool in the grateful room
In which, like branches on related trees,
They stirred towards each other, touched and clung,
Awed by the haunting music that was sung.

A Quaint Disorder

A quaint disorder, this:
I do not sleep too well
For fear the dark hours build
A solitary cell;
My intellect expels
Its former policies,
Disburdened can explore
Remoter galaxies.
My heart snarls at the way
The minutes pitter past
Towards the last abyss.
I tremble at the vast
Arsenals that Chance
Commands, could call upon
To lay mines in your path.
The moonlight that once shone
Benignly frightens me,
As does deceitful air;
Time's frequent felonies
Are crueller than they were.
Food no longer tempts
The withered appetite;
I hunger only for
That longed-for good tonight
When you, desired physician,
Will come with healing art
And magical prescription
To purge my febrile heart

Of all its grave distempers
And burn my fever-chart.
A quaint disorder, this,
Which stabs with hope and doubt,
And one – with all its pains –
I would not be without.

Growing Pain

The boy was barely five years old.
We sent him to the little school
And left him there to learn the names
Of flowers in jam jars on the sill
And learn to do as he was told.
He seemed quite happy there until
Three weeks afterwards, at night,
The darkness whimpered in his room.
I went upstairs, switched on his light,
And found him wide awake, distraught,
Sheets mangled and his eiderdown
Untidy carpet on the floor.
I said, 'Why can't you sleep? A pain?'
He snuffled, gave a little moan,
And then he spoke a single word:
'Jessica.' The sound was blurred.
'Jessica? What do you mean?'
'A girl at school called Jessica,
She hurts –' he touched himself between
The heart and stomach '– she has been
Aching here and I can see her.'
Nothing I had read or heard
Instructed me in what to do.
I covered him and stroked his head.
'The pain will go, in time,' I said.

Blood Letter

Frail leech that craves an open vein,
Paper vampire, blood-letter,
Go in your mild envelope
Disguised as harmless paper.

Dissemble in the postman's sack,
Mix with football coupons, views
Of beaches, blackmail, racing tips,
Poems and domestic news.

Go to her whose heart your need is,
But temper your red hunger, rest
Gently on her pulses, be
Tender at her breast.

And hope that she will welcome you
To ease her fever and make better
Such distemper as she suffers,
Letter of blood, love-letter.

Incendiary

That one small boy with a face like pallid cheese
And burnt-out little eyes could make a blaze
As brazen, fierce and huge, as red and gold
And zany yellow as the one that spoiled
Three thousand guineas' worth of property
And crops at Godwin's Farm on Saturday
Is frightening – as fact and metaphor.
An ordinary match intended for
The lighting of a pipe or kitchen fire
Misused may set a whole menagerie
Of flame-fanged tigers roaring hungrily.
And frightening, too, that one small boy should set
The sky on fire and choke the stars to heat
Such skinny limbs and such a little heart
Which would have been content with one warm kiss
Had there been anyone to offer this.

A Song to Celebrate

Your hair tastes of darkness.
The sea fondles the long drowned.
The shore extends a delicate limb,
The waves relish its whiteness.

Your mouth tastes of moonlight.
The city revs its dark engines;
Lamps are bright burs on the night's coat.
I would wear you like a cloak

And would be your robe for all weathers.
Your flesh tastes of sunlight.
The sea concedes defeat. The drowned
Rise white and dance naked.

No Sense of Direction

I have always admired
Those who are sure
Which turning to take,
Who need no guide
Even in war
When thunders shake
The torn terrain,
When battalions of shrill
Stars all desert
And the derelict moon
Goes over the hill:
Eyes chained by the night
They find their way back
As if it were daylight.
Then, on peaceful walks
Over strange wooded ground,
They will find the right track,
Know which of the forks
Will lead to the inn
I would never have found;
For I lack their gift,
Possess almost no
Sense of direction.
And yet I owe
A debt to this lack,
A debt so vast
No reparation
Can ever be made,

For it led me away
From the road I sought
Which would carry me to –
I mistakenly thought –
My true destination:
It made me stray
To this lucky path
That ran like a fuse
And brought me to you
And love's bright, soundless
Detonation.

Summer in the Park

Sun leans lightly on all temples;
In the park the far trees
Melt at their shadowed knees.
Summer supplies its simples
For all but one disease:
Young dogs, young sons, young mothers,
Gold waterfall hair of daughters
Float over trim green seas.
He could munch them up and swallow them,
Yes, even the melting trees,
The staid man on the seat
Whose heart's teeth ache with love
And its impossible sweet.

A Love Song

I've always been in love with you I swear.
'Impossible,' they say, yet it is true:
I speak with certainty, for I was there.

When I reeled groggy as the punchbowl air
Was spiced with melody I longed for you;
I've always been in love with you I swear.

My infant whispers to the beat-up bear
Were meant for you, the tears and kisses too;
I speak with certainty, for I was there.

Let experts, calendars and maps declare
I'm nuts or have at least one wobbly screw;
I've always been in love with you I swear.

New kinds of beauty and the wish to share
These riches were rehearsals, as I knew,
I speak with certainty, for I was there.

Those shadow-loves were work-outs to prepare
For this, the main event, that they led to:
I've always been in love with you I swear;
I speak with certainty, for I was there.

Nightsong

Tonight the dark is wild:
It thumps on silence with blind fists;
In its head the fog-horns moan.
Out there at sea,
Its rage infects the waves.
They could be strangling deck-hands,
Lambasting bosuns, gulping stewards;
Yet here we are, secure and warm,
Though not entirely dry.

Oh my love, that moistness,
Small sargasso,
The swell and heave and hunger
Will devour, devour.
Dear carnivore, my child, my world,
The night is wild.

The Loving Game

A quarter of a century ago
I hung the gloves up, knew I'd had enough
Of taking it and trying to dish it out,
Foxing them or slugging toe-to-toe;
Keen youngsters made the going a bit too rough;
The time had come to have my final bout.

I didn't run to fat though, kept in shape,
And seriously took up the loving game,
Grew moony, sighed, and even tried to sing,
Looked pretty snappy in my forty-drape.
I lost more than I won, earned little fame,
Was hurt much worse than in the other ring.

Wicket Maiden

It is a game for gentle men;
Entirely wrong that man's spare rib
Should learn the mysteries of spin.

Women should not be allowed
To study subtleties of flight;
They should bowl underarm and wide.

Or better still, not bowl at all,
Sit elegant in summer chairs,
Flatter the quiet with pale applause.

It shouldn't happen, yet it did:
She bowled a wicked heartbreak – one,
That's all. God help the next man in.

Simplicities

Now that you have gone
I feel a compulsion to write
not literature but something quite
private, for your eyes only to look upon.

It is good for once,
to ignore the demands of art,
utter simplicities of the heart
and happily become your passionate dunce.

Yet instinct compels
me to accept a formal task;
speech from behind ceremony's mask
might chime with the truth and music of bright bells.

So I have chosen
a syllabic measure this time,
linking these awkward lines with a rhyme-
pattern borrowed from Alfred, Lord Tennyson.

All I wish to do
though is something simple as this:
tell you how I still taste your last kiss,
and say, like any dunce, how much I love you.

Company of Women

I
Miss Steeples

Miss Steeples sat close;
She touched me.
Her hands were white,
Fingernails pink
Like shells of prawns.
They tapped my desk
And, as she murmured,
Numbers blurred.
She smelled of spring
And cool cash chemists.
One summer evening,
Not by chance,
I met her walking
Near the green
Court she beautified
Dressed in white.
In one hand swung
A netted catch
Of tennis balls.
She smiled and said,
'Hello.'
She smiled.
Love-punctured
I could not answer.
At the end of the summer

She went away.
It was her smell I loved
And her fingernails.

II
Thelma

Thelma was a Brownie.
I never spoke to her
Although we spent a year together
In Standard Three.
I once followed her home
From the Brownie HQ.
There was honeysuckle in the gardens;
Songs of gramophones, too.
The satchel she brought to school
Was made of expensive leather
And in her hair
She wore a slide of tortoiseshell,
My first fetish.
We never spoke,
Not once in all that time.
It was a long spell
And is not over:
When I smell honeysuckle now
It is Thelma I smell.

III
Doris

Doris was fifteen.
Under her unsuitable blouse
Her breasts bounced when she ran.
I kissed her once
And she fled
Giggling and joggling home.
MacFeeney cheered like a football crowd.
I made his nose bleed.
Doris was more exciting
Than cigarettes,
Sweeter than caramels,
More sparkling than sherbet.
For thirteen weeks I saved
To buy her a gift:
It looked like a sucked pear-drop
On a thin chain.
I like to think of it, snug
Between those plump bubs,
Those joys
That age has never withered.
MacFeeney keeps a pub in Mablethorpe.

IV
Kathleen

Kathleen was tall.
My eyes grew dizzy when they climbed
Her legs;
Sometimes they fell.
Her hair was rich
And golden red,
It glowed like fire
Reflected in
Good marmalade.
We walked at night
Under a nervous sky,
Its darkness probed and drenched
By searchlights, jets
Of phosphorescent milk
Thrilling the black air.
Marauding engines grumbled
As we played
With high explosives
Of primed limbs and lips;
Incendiary kisses fell.
My hands grew dizzy when they climbed
Her legs
But did not fall.
At her long cry
All sirens held their tongues.
Her hair was drenched, it spread
Wild and impenitent,
A red and morning cloud
Above a wasted town
That smouldered but already stirred,
Would rise up new again.

V
Barbara

Barbara was small
But in that little space
A charge of sexual voltage hummed
And, when released, it singed and dazzled mad.
I gave her poetry to read:
She judged it 'very nice',
Would rather far
Been offered chocolate or kisses.
One winter night, the pubs all shut,
She crouched beneath the frosty stars
And pissed.
She looked up, grinning, as the glitter hissed.
And that is what I most remember,
Less passion than delight,
More mischief than dark moans –
Quick sparkle, hiss and rising mist,
The frosty stars
And Barbara twinkling wantonly
And wild.

The Widow's Complaint

You left as you so often left before,
Sneaking out on tiptoe,
No slam of door,
Off to drink with enemies of mine,
And of yours –
If you could only see it –
Drunkards and bores
Whose grossest flatteries
You swilled down with the booze
That you never had the gumption to refuse.
You won't come back this time.
No need to prepare
A welcome for you – clamped silence
And belligerent stare –
No need for morning nostrums or to hide
The whisky and car-keys,
Tighten my lips and thighs
Against your pleas,
No need for those old stratagems any more.
But you might have let me know what was in store;
Your last low trick
To leave me with no clue
That you had gone for good,
My last chance lost
To tell you what I've so long wanted to
How much I hate you and I always have,
You pig, you bastard,

Stinking rat –
Oh, love, my love,
How can I forgive you that?

When We Were Married

She took the book from the shelf
And turned the pages slowly.
'I loved this book,' she said,
'When we were married.

'That song that teases silence
Was a favourite of mine;
It did not grow tedious
While we were married.

'I ate some food tonight
But did not relish it.
It was a dish that I enjoyed
When we were married.

'When we were married,' she said,
And her lashes were glistening,
'I felt at home in this house, that bed.'
But the man was not listening.

Desirable Residence

They came quick stepping, laughing lively,
Loving hands held warm and tightly;
Their eyes were ripe and bright,
And both were handsome in their light
Suits of youth. Her walk was dance
And his quick march.
They mocked the staid with stance and glance,
And then they paused outside the house,
Admired its pretty clothes,
The shine and sparkle and the green
Apron fringed with rose.
Each faced the other, smiled, and then,
Still holding hands, clicked smartly in;
And they were never seen again.

Questions About Paradise

Did it rain in the Garden of Eden?
Did original man and his mate
improvise leafy umbrellas
and wait for the storm to abate?

Was it chilly at night in the Garden?
Did they shiver with cold as they lay
huddled together in bracken,
longing for temperate day?

And what did they have for their breakfast?
What would Eve rustle up there to eat?
It wouldn't be kidneys or bacon
for they neither, surely, ate meat.

They might have drunk something like coffee
or tea but, more probably milk.
They didn't wear clothes for adornment
or warmth, neither cotton nor silk.

Did they fuck before eating the apple?
The Bible on this isn't clear;
they certainly did after sentence
or else you and I'd not be here.

But how did they talk to each other,
to God and the serpent as well?
They must have commanded a language
to speak with, if not write and spell.

It is true that the word 'prelapsarian'
connotes a past heavenly state,
yet it seems that those two vegetarian
nudists chose outside the Gate.

For while they were stuck in the Garden,
life surely was terribly bleak,
just the two with so little to talk of,
if indeed they were able to speak.

Their lives were devoid of all passion
and contrast and music and art,
ignorant of love and the secret
dark galleries deep in the heart.

It was Eve, with her feminine instinct
for the basics, who well understood
to be human you have to discover
the nature of evil and good,

and that beauty, love and fulfilment
are conditional, not dished out free,
contingent on time and on hazard,
and on Death's stern necessity.

Five Versions of Rimbaud

I
OPHELIA

On the tranquil black river where dreaming stars rest
Ophelia floats slowly, liliaceously pale
On her long wavering veils; from the woods in the west
Sound the horn-notes of hunters saluting their kill.

For more than a thousand sad years she has drifted,
white phantom afloat on the endless dark river,
and all through that time her sweet madness has whispered
its tale to the breeze-troubled willows that shiver.

The amorous wind is caressing her bosom
and it gently unfolds her white veils in a wreath
that lifts and subsides to the river's slow rhythm;
the willows arch over and weep out their grief.

Water-lilies also draw close and are sighing,
and sometimes her passing elicits from leaves
brief flutter of wings discreetly applauding
the shimmering music the night sky achieves.

*

O pale Ophelia, beautiful as snow,
you died and were borne by the river away;
it was winds from the white peaks of Norway that brought
    you
both the message of freedom and the price you must pay.

And the wind in your hair breathed those rumours that
    stirred
such dark pertubations of spirit and mind;
your tender heart listened to Nature and heard
the night's trembling sigh and the great trees that groaned.

It was the roar of the lunatic ocean that broke
your vulnerable spirit, soft heart of a child;
and the poor mad prince who, unable to speak
on that morning in April, saw you beguiled.

What a rich dream of love and freedom, mad girl!
He was the fire, and you melted like snow;
your vision's great glory choked back all the words;
infinity dazzled and stunned like a blow.

                    *

And the poet has told us that now you come seeking
by starlight the flowers you once gathered with care;
and again he has seen, in her long veils reclining,
the lily Ophelia, still beautiful there.

                    *

II
A Winter Dream

In winter we'll ride in a small railway carriage
    with pink decor and cushions of blue;
in each cosy corner a nest of wild kisses
    to be plundered by me and by you.

You will close your bright eyes against prowling shadows
    that bring, in the darkness, vile shapes,
which, glaring and snarling, press close to the windows,
    monsters that no one escapes.

Then, light as a spider, my delicate kisses
will tickle your cheek like an insect that passes
    on to your neck where you'll feel

its journeying downwards. 'Oh help! I beseech you!'
you'll cry as, together, we search for this creature
    well-known for exploratory zeal.

III
The First Evening

She was half-dressed, or less than half.
Great voyeuristic trees outside
pressed their leaves against the glass,
slyly pushing, spreading wide.

Half-naked in my chair's embrace
she sat, with both hands clasped together.
Her little feet showed such sweet grace,
trembling on the floor with pleasure.

I saw a little beam of light,
waxen-tinted, playing over
her smiling lips and on the white
curve of breast, a fly on roses.

I kissed her dainty ankles. She
laughed, at first a soft low note
which then rose bright and trillingly,
crystalline from her arched throat.

Her small feet hid beneath frail tent
of petticoat. 'Do stop!' she cried,
her laugh pretended punishment
for what in fact she had desired.

I softly kissed her trembling eyes
that fluttered under my warm lips.
She moved her head away and sighed:
'I think this far enough, perhaps ...

'I've things to say, so listen sir...'
I moved my lips from eyes to breast,
and, as I kissed and fondled her,
her throaty laugh held no protest.

She was half-dressed, or less than half.
Great voyeuristic trees outside
pressed their leaves against the glass,
slyly pushing, spreading wide.

IV
The Lice Hunters

When the child's head is tortured by red
malice of lice, he yearns for the white
calm solace of dreams, but now in its stead
come his two lovely sisters, nails silvery bright.

They seat him in front of the wide open casement
where blue air is scented by cocktails of flowers
and the night-dew descends, anointing his opulent
locks where their fingers are magical prowlers.

He hears the soft sighs of their vigilant breathing
which carries the honey-sweet fragrance of roses,
broken at times by a salivary hissing
from lips moist for kissing, a sound that bemuses.

He can hear, too, their eyelashes beat in the silence
like dark wings of insects; he feels their slim fingers,
electrically thrilling, passing death-sentence;
hears tiny explosions, minikin angers.

And then the child feels a deep langour steal over
all senses, a cloaking melodious sigh;
those fingers, caressing, induce a strange fever,
mysterious tristesse, a compulsion to cry.

V
The Sleeper in the Valley

A grassy hollow with a lilting river
which scatters its silvery shreds on the reeds
as the sun from the hills sets the calm air aquiver
with shimmering light that floods and recedes:

a young and bare-headed soldier sleeps there;
his lips are apart, cress cool on the skin
of vulnerable neck; he lies in the glare
and waterless drizzle of afternoon sun.

His feet in the tall yellow irises rest
and he smiles like a child at his mother's soft breast;
O, cradle him gently in arms warm and wide.

He is cold and his delicate nostrils are closed
to sonatas of fragrance that Summer's composed.
Two crimson holes have been punched in his side.

The Year of the Crab

Intimations of Mortality

In fading English summer where, quite soon,
the wistful autumn would begin its fall
before the winter bared its moon-white fangs,
he planned escape from winds that pierce and hurt:
he booked a flight to a winterless land
of speedwell sky and vanilla sand.
Already, though, a vague discomfort stirred;
pain's pallid shadow and its soundless trill
flickered in his throat.
                        The Doctor said
'It's thrush,' and gave him lozenges to suck.
The ache remained. Again, the same prescription,
but no change; slight darkening of the shade perhaps,
invading places other than the flesh.

Weeks sidled past; leaves crisped and floated down,
slithering in the soupy air. The ancient scents
of autumn bonfires came and went.
The Doctor frowned, more puzzled than alarmed,
and sent him to a specialist who found
no thrush had nested snug in his warm throat,
no feathered flutter, but the hard-clawed crab.

The plane for warm escape stayed on the ground.

. . . .

The words were heard and understood:
no knife-blade shock. It seemed as if
some half-expected news had come at last.

And so the measured processes began
which brought him here, to winter and this bed,
where neutered and more neatly parcelled than
ever at home in longed-for, shared domain
of love and sleep, he looks around and sees
the so-far nameless others, like himself embossed
along the margins of the ward, each one a word,
synonymous, not quick or lumbering verb,
but each a hybrid vocable, half adjective, half noun,
a 'patient' – and, inertly patient, he
and everyone of them would have to be.

Choice, with their outdoor clothing, has been locked
    away.

He cannot move, except inside his head
where move he does, not far in time or space,
a few weeks only, travelling in reverse
to when he was escorted to the 'Mould Room' for
the fitting of his plastic 'shell', or 'mask'.
Warm bandages were wound about his head and neck
until his face was covered save for holes
cut out for eyes and mouth. He thought
that he must be a sight to terrify
the young or, to the old, bring images
in black and white of H.G. Wells's Man
beneath whose bandages were nothingness and night.

The cast of head and neck set hard;
from this the mask or shell was shaped.
Next came the X-rays, then the 'Simulation'
when radiotherapy's procedures were rehearsed:
they stretched him out on what they called the 'couch'

on which the glassy shell of plastic which contained
his captive head was firmly clamped,
immovable, beneath the engine's steady hum:
all music killed, all singing dumb,
frivolities of far-off pleasures drilled
by that thin driving sound. The plastic shell
became a world of glass, his skull
its sole inhabitant, fixed firm and still
as specimen in laboratory or museum.

After this the real thing could begin.

The Machine Room

This scene, to a neutrally cool gaze, might seem
like footage from an early film, Fritz Lang perhaps,
an unmade movie mixing modes –
a quasi-scientific vision of a world
in black and white, mysterious machines,
attendant figures, sacerdotal, gowned,
and a horror film in which the home-made man
is yet to rise from where he lies, strapped down,
to set about his mad creators and rove wild.
But, to the patient in his vitreous world,
stretched on his trestle-bed, the room
is sounds of movement, mechanical and alive,
steely sighs and groans, a steady hum,
then conference of voices, low, intent,
discussing problems in their unknown tongue
while he, like his own grandchild, listens to
the serious grown-up sounds that make no sense.

Darkness and light perform their dance.
He counts masked seconds as they shuffle past
and waits for his release.
He prays that he will neither sneeze nor cough.

Then, with unexpected and explosive crash,
the plastic shell containing neck and head
is – as always, shockingly – unclamped,
and he is helped by practised hands
down from the narrow couch to stand
restored to a brief and dizzy perpendicular
before being lowered to his patient chair
and wheeled away towards the ward
to lie and wait until the following day's
confinement in the glassy cranial cell.

The Treatment

Day after aching day, week after clubfoot week,
the course of radiation moved
towards its fifth and final week;
and now, at last, the daily treatments done,
he wears a scarf of stinging-nettles
tight about his throat.
His mouth, a little dungeon, dark and dry,
is haunted by the vile, insistent shade
of putrefying fish; a slender tube
creeps up one nostril and descends
to unprotesting stomach to convey
some tasteless stuff that holds him down to earth.

He hears faint fluttering reports
of snow and early dark, and longs for her
to bring that perfect sweetness to the heart's
unsullied palate and the faint,
remembered fragrance of her wake.

Loving the Nurses

Slowly, the long pale bandage of each day
unwinds and darkens as the night descends;
hygienic and efficient hands bring opiates
and pain slinks off to its hot lair.
He feels for every nurse a blend
of gratitude and admiration that, together, ape
the lineaments of love; he has read somewhere
all patients fall in love with those who wear
the uniform of trained compassion; now he learns
that this is almost true, though 'almost' rules
with that authority which overturns
the absolute of 'true' as his true love
comes in from loveless night and brings those spoils
which neither he nor his affliction earns.

Night Shift

Well past midnight now: outside,
beyond these still curtains, heavy with implications,
their secretive corrugations,
the wind whimpers and whispers to be let in.

A single circular lamp, stunned moon,
flat on the ceiling, dilutes the dark
but cannot cancel it. The quietness
is never absolute; sleep crumples it.

The sighs and snarls of human breathing
seem no more meaningful than the wind's noise
or the faraway whispering of a nurse:
her voice is a tuneless lullaby.

At spaced intervals the figures move,
sexless in their long vague robes,
slow and soundless down the ward,
anonymous and self-absorbed.

The pale procession will last as long
as darkness lasts. They have lost
their ordinariness with their identities.
They are practising at being ghosts.

Morning Shift

After the gaunt night, its taut sheet
of silence torn from time to time
by sudden cries and the urgent morse

of hurrying feet, the hushed confabulations,
darkness clinging still to outer panes
behind the brooding curtains,

comes the time of neither night nor sunrise,
a brief, noiseless lacuna of exhaustion,
before the morning shift arrives,

not seen as yet, but audible,
an awakening of starlings and sparrows,
laughter, voices, the cold scent of dew and dawn,

a distant whisper of wind in shivering leaves,
a rumour of drenched petals unfolding:
morning puts on its fresh starched uniform.

Going Home

The daily dosages of radiation are now finished.
External and internal flesh of throat and neck
simmers with sores. The marvel, Morphine, holds
the pain away. He has not swallowed food or drink
for months; the nasogastric tube is still in place,
it trails, escaped spaghetti, from his nose
to be attached to feeding-pump four times each day.
His love learns from the nurses how to handle this,
what drugs and in what quantities to give,
and then he is released to leave for home
where all his nursing will be done
by unofficial care which, uncomplaining, works
on every shift with only gratitude for wage.

Although it takes stretched months
and two returns to hospital before
he can attempt to eat as others do,
the time draws slowly closer and, at last, he hears,
if only faintly, that low growl and purr
of powerful aero-engines, fuelled now
for long-delayed escape to winter warmth,
the land where orange-blossom stains soft air
when sleet and snow enshroud the fields of home,
a place of soft, slow rhythms, real Cockaigne
which not long since, in misery and pain,
he feared that he would never see again.

Postscript: Andalusian Afternoon

In the narrow street between the tall
white buildings with jet iron traceries
and whispered secrecies of glass,
which tell you nothing though they hint
at sensuous possibilities, dark shadows slant
and splash on wall and paving-stone. Two children
are laughing as they play with a large black dog
and a pink balloon, while he and she
look down, unseen, from their small balcony.

Behind them, still and cool, the room recalls
once more a Schubert Trio in B Flat
and, as the Scherzo dances, the black dog bounds
and pounces on the light pink globe
of air held tight in shining weightless skin
which quite astounds by bouncing free,
unpunctured by the canine claws,
and, teasing, settles only feet away.
Delighted squeals float up like small balloons.

And this slight incident, without intent,
is beautiful, this moment in a burnished afternoon
in a lofty room in Southern Spain
will be remembered with that nimble tune,
black glossiness of dog and pink balloon,
and if a whisper of uncertainty is heard
between the scherzo and the rondo it affords
a glint of seasoning, a piquancy,
which makes the mortal moment more their own.